The Women Who Came In The Mayflower

by

Annie Russell Marble

The Women Who Came
In The Mayflower
by Annie Russell Marble

ISBN: 978-93-59328-57-7

Published by

DOUBLE 9 BOOKS

2/13-B, Ansari Road
Daryaganj, New Delhi – 110002
info@double9books.com
www.double9books.com
Tel. 011-40042856

ABOUT THE AUTHOR

A pioneer of the transcendental movement and a well acclaimed novelist in America, Annie Russell Marble primarily wrote about early American historical personalities. She also provided analysis on literature generally. She was Isaiah Dunster Russell's child. In 1882, she graduated from Worcester High School and went on to earn an MA at Smith College. In addition to the publications listed below, she also wrote numerous essays on early American history and literature and published a number of calendars and almanacks with a literary theme. This was preceded by a few magazine articles. She served as the Worcester Sunday Telegram's literary editor and book critic from 1920 to 1929.

CONTENTS

FOREWORD

This little book is intended as a memorial to the women who came in *The Mayflower*, and their comrades who came later in *The Ann* and *The Fortune*, who maintained the high standards of home life in early Plymouth Colony. There is no attempt to make a genealogical study of any family. The effort is to reveal glimpses of the communal life during 1621-1623. This is supplemented by a few silhouettes of individual matrons and maidens to whose influence we may trace increased resources in domestic life and education.

One must regret the lack of proof regarding many facts, about which are conflicting statements, both of the general conditions and the individual men and women. In some instances, both points of view have been given here; at other times, the more probable surmises have been mentioned.

The author feels deep gratitude, and would here express it, to the librarians of the Massachusetts Historical Society, the New England Genealogic-Historical Register, the American Antiquarian Society, the Register of Deeds, Pilgrim Hall, and the Russell Library of Plymouth, private and public libraries of Duxbury and Marshfield, and to Mr. Arthur Lord and all other individuals who have assisted in this research. The publications of the Society of Mayflower Descendants, and the remarkable researches of its editor, Mr. George E. Bowman, call for special appreciation.

ANNIE RUSSELL MARBLE. *Worcester, Massachusetts.*

CHAPTER I
ENDURANCE AND ADVENTURE:
THE VOYAGE AND LANDING

"So they left ye goodly and pleasante citie, which had been ther resting-place near 12 years; but they knew they were pilgrimes, & looked not much on those things, but lift up their eyes to ye heavens, their dearest cuntrie, and quieted their spirits."

—Bradford's History of Plymouth Plantations. Chap. VII.

December weather in New England, even at its best, is a test of physical endurance. With warm clothes and sheltering homes today, we find compensations for the cold winds and storms in the exhilarating winter sports and the good cheer of the holiday season.

The passengers of *The Mayflower* anchored in Plymouth harbor, three hundred years ago, lacked compensations of sports or fireside warmth. One hundred and two in number when they sailed,—of whom twenty-nine were women,—they had been crowded for ten weeks into a vessel that was intended to carry about half the number of passengers. In low spaces between decks, with some fine weather when the open hatchways allowed air to enter and more stormy days when they were shut in amid discomforts of all kinds, they had come at last within sight of the place where, contrary to their plans, they were destined to make their settlement.

At Plymouth, England, their last port in September, they had "been kindly entertained and courteously used by divers friends there dwelling," [Footnote: Relation or Journal of a Plantation Settled at Plymouth in New-England and Proceedings Thereof; London, 1622 (Bradford and Winslow) Abbreviated In Purchas' Pilgrim, X; iv; London, 1625.] but they were homeless now, facing a new country with frozen shores, menaced by wild animals and yet more fearsome savages. Whatever trials of their good sense and sturdy faith came later, those days of waiting until shelter could be raised on shore, after the weeks of confinement, must have challenged their physical and spiritual fortitude.

There must have been exciting days for the women on shipboard and in landing. There must have been hours of distress for the older and the delight in adventure which is an unchanging trait of the young of every race. Wild winds carried away some clothes and cooking-dishes from the ship; there was a birth and a death, and occasional illness, besides the dire seasickness. John Howland, "the lustie young man," fell overboard but he caught hold of the topsail halyard which hung extended and so held on "though he was sundry fathoms under water," until he was pulled up by a rope and rescued by a boat-hook. [Footnote: Bradford's History of Plymouth Plantation; ch. 9.]

Recent research [Footnote: "The Mayflower," by H. G. Marsden; Eng. Historical Review, Oct., 1904; The Mayflower Descendant, Jan., 1916] has argued that the captain of *The Mayflower* was probably not *Thomas Jones*, with reputation for severity, but a Master Christopher Jones of kindlier temper. The former captain was in Virginia, in September, 1620, according to this account. With the most generous treatment which the captain and crew could give to the women, they must have been sorely tried. There were sick to be nursed, children to be cared for, including some lively boys who played with powder and nearly caused an explosion at Cape Cod; nourishment must be found for all from a store of provisions that had been much reduced by the delays and necessary sales to satisfy their "merchant adventurers" before they left England. They slept on damp bedding and wore musty clothes; they lacked exercise and water for drink or cleanliness. Joyful for them must have been the day recorded by Winslow and Bradford, [Footnote: Relation or Journal, etc. (1622).]—"On Monday the thirteenth of November our people went on shore to refresh themselves and our women to wash, as they had great need."

During the anxious days when the abler men were searching on land for a site for the settlement, first on Cape Cod and later at Plymouth, there were events of excitement on the ship left in the harbor. Peregrine White was born and his father's servant, Edward Thompson, died. Dorothy May Bradford, the girl-wife of the later Governor of the colony, was drowned during his absence. There were murmurings and threats against the leaders by some of the crew and others who were impatient at the long voyage, scant comforts and uncertain future. Possibly some of the complaints came from women, but in the hearts of most of them, although no women signed their names, was the resolution that inspired the men who signed that compact in the cabin of *The Mayflower*,—"to promise all due submission and obedience." They had pledged their "great hope and inward zeal of laying good foundation for ye propagating and advancing ye gospell of ye kingdom of Christ in those remote parts of ye world; yea, though they should be but as stepping-stones unto others for ye performing of so great a work"; with such spirit they had been impelled to leave Holland and such faith sustained them on their long journey.

Many of the women who were pioneers at Plymouth had suffered severe hardships in previous years. They could sustain their own hearts and encourage the younger ones by remembrance of the passage from England to Holland, twelve years before, when they were searched most cruelly, even deprived of their clothes and belongings by the ship's master at Boston. Later they were abandoned by the Dutchman at Hull, to wait for fourteen days of frightful storm while their husbands and protectors were carried far away in a ship towards the coast of Norway, "their little ones hanging about them and quaking with cold." [Footnote: Bradford's History of Plymouth Plantation; ch. 2.]

There were women with frail bodies, like Rose Standish and Katherine Carver, but there were strong physiques and dauntless hearts sustained to great old age, matrons like Susanna White and Elizabeth Hopkins and young women like Priscilla Mullins, Mary Chilton, Elizabeth Tilley and Constance Hopkins. In our imaginations today, few women correspond to the clinging, fainting figures portrayed by some of the painters of "The Departure" or "The Landing of the Pilgrims." We may more readily believe that most of the women were upright and alert, peering anxiously but courageously into the future. Writing in 1910, John Masefield said: [Footnote: Introduction to Chronicles of the Pilgrim Fathers (Everyman's Library).] "A generation fond of pleasure, disinclined towards serious thought, and shrinking from hardship, even if it may be swiftly reached, will find it difficult to imagine the temper, courage and manliness of the emigrants who made the first Christian settlement of New England." Ten years ago it would have been as difficult for women of our day to understand adequately the womanliness of the Pilgrim matrons and girls. The anxieties and self-denials experienced by women of all lands during the last five years may help us to "imagine" better the dauntless spirit of these women of New-Plymouth. During those critical months of 1621-1623 they sustained their households and assisted the men in establishing an orderly and religious colony. We may justly affirm that some of "the wisdom, prudence and patience and just and equall carriage of things by the better part" [Footnote: Bradford's History of Plymouth Plantation; Bk. II.] was manifested among the women as well as the men.

In spite of the spiritual zeal which comes from devotion to a good cause, and the inspiration of steady work, the women must have suffered from homesickness, as well as from anxiety and illness. They had left in Holland not alone their loved pastor, John Robinson, and their valiant friend,

Robert Cushman, but many fathers, mothers, brothers and sisters besides their "dear gossips." Mistress Brewster yearned for her elder son and her daughters, Fear and Patience; Priscilla Mullins and Mary Chilton, soon to be left orphans, had been separated from older brothers and sisters. Disease stalked among them on land and on shipboard like a demon. Before the completion of more than two or three of the one-room, thatched houses, the deaths were multiplying. Possibly this disease was typhus fever; more probably it was a form of infectious pneumonia, due to enervated conditions of the body and to exposures at Cape Cod. Winslow declared, in his account of the expedition on shore, "It blowed and did snow all that day and night and froze withal. Some of our people that are dead took the original of their death there." Had the disease been "galloping consumption," as has been suggested sometimes, it is not probable that many of those "sick unto death" would have recovered and have lived to be octogenarians.

The toll of deaths increased and the illness spread until, at one time, there were only "six or seven sound persons" to minister to the sick and to bury the dead. Fifteen of the twenty-nine women who sailed from England and Holland were buried on Plymouth hillside during the winter and spring. They were: Rose Standish; Elizabeth, wife of Edward Winslow; Mary, wife of Isaac Allerton; Sarah, wife of Francis Eaton; Katherine, wife of Governor John Carver; Alice, wife of John Rigdale; Ann, wife of Edward Fuller; Bridget and Ann Tilley, wives of John and Edward; Alice, wife of John Mullins or Molines; Mrs. James Chilton; Mrs. Christopher Martin; Mrs. Thomas Tinker; possibly Mrs. John Turner, and Ellen More, the orphan ward of Edward Winslow. Nearly twice as many men as women died during those fateful months of 1621. Can we "imagine" the courage required by the few women who remained after this devastation, as the wolves were heard howling in the night, the food supplies were fast disappearing, and the houses of shelter were delayed in completion by "frost and much foul weather," and by the very few men in physical condition to rive timber or to thatch roofs? The common house, twenty foot square, was crowded with the sick, among them Carver and Bradford, who were obliged "to rise in good speed" when the roof caught on fire, and their loaded muskets in rows beside the beds threatened an explosion. [Footnote: Mourt's Relation.]

Although the women's strength of body and soul must have been sapped yet their fidelity stood well the test; when *The Mayflower* was to return to England in April and the captain offered free passage to the women as well as to any men who wished to go, if the women "would cook and nurse such of the crew as were ill," not a man or a woman accepted the offer. Intrepid in bravery and faith, the women did their part in making this lonely, impoverished settlement into a home. This required adjustments of many kinds. Few in number, the women represented distinctive classes of society in birth and education. In Leyden, for seven years, they had chosen their friends and there they formed a happy community, in spite of some poverty and more anxiety about the education and morals of their children, because of "the manifold temptations" [Footnote: Bradford's History of Plymouth Plantation, ch. 3.] of the Dutch city.

Many of the men, on leaving England, had renounced their more leisurely occupations and professions to practise trades in Leyden,—Brewster and Winslow as printers, Allerton as tailor, Dr. Samuel Fuller as say-weaver and others as carpenters, wool-combers, masons, cobblers, pewterers and in other crafts. A few owned residences near the famous University of Leyden, where Robinson and Brewster taught. Some educational influences would thus fall upon their families. [Footnote: The England and Holland of the Pilgrims, Henry M. Dexter and Morton Dexter, Boston, 1905.] On the other hand, others were recorded as "too poor to be taxed." Until July, 1620, there were two hundred and ninety-eight known members of this church in Leyden with nearly three hundred more associated with them. Such economic and social conditions gave to the women certain privileges and pleasures in addition to the interesting events in this picturesque city.

In *The Mayflower* and at Plymouth, on the other hand, the women were thrust into a small company with widely differing tastes and backgrounds. One of the first demands made upon them was for a democratic spirit,— tolerance and patience, adaptability to varied natures. The old joke that "the Pilgrim Mothers had to endure not alone their hardships but the Pilgrim Fathers also" has been overworked. These women would never have accepted pity as martyrs. They came to this new country with devotion to the men of their families and, in those days, such a call was supreme in a woman's life. They sorrowed for the women friends who had been left behind,—the wives of Dr. Fuller, Richard Warren, Francis Cooke and Degory Priest, who were to come later after months of anxious waiting for a message from New-Plymouth.

The family, not the individual, characterized the life of that community. The father was always regarded as the "head" of the family. Evidence of this is found when we try to trace the posterity of some of the pioneer women from the Old Plymouth Colony Records. A child is there recorded as "the son of Nicholas Snow," "the son of John Winslow" or "the daughter of Thomas Cushman" with no hint that the mothers of these children were, respectively, Constance Hopkins, Mary Chilton and Mary Allerton, all of whom came in *The Mayflower*, although the fathers arrived at Plymouth later on *The Fortune* and *The Ann*.

It would be unjust to assume that these women were conscious heroines. They wrought with courage and purpose equal to these traits in the men, but probably none of the Pilgrims had a definite vision of the future. With words of appreciation that are applicable to both sexes, ex-President Charles W. Eliot has said: [Footnote: Eighteenth Annual Dinner of Mayflower Society, Nov. 20, 1913.] "The Pilgrims did not know the issue and they had no vision of it. They just loved liberty and toleration and truth, and hoped for more of it, for more liberty, for a more perfect toleration, for more truth, and they put their lives, their labors, at the disposition of those loves without the least vision of this republic, or of what was going to come out of their industry, their devotion, their dangerous and exposed lives."

CHAPTER II
COMMUNAL AND FAMILY LIFE
IN PLYMOUTH 1621-1623

Spring and summer came to bless them for their endurance and unconscious heroism. Then they could appreciate the verdict of their leaders, who chose the site of Plymouth as a "hopeful place," with running brooks, vines of sassafras and strawberry, fruit trees, fish and wild fowl and "clay excellent for pots and will wash like soap." [Footnote: Mourt's Relation] So early was the spring in 1621 that on March the third there was a thunder storm and "the birds sang in the woods most pleasantly." On March the sixteenth, Samoset came with Indian greeting. This visit must have been one of mixed sentiments for the women and we can read more than the mere words in the sentence, "We lodged him that night at Stephen Hopkins' house and watched him." [Footnote: Mourt's Relation.] Perhaps it was in deference to the women that the men gave Samoset a hat, a pair of stockings, shoes, a shirt and a piece of cloth to tie about his waist. Samoset returned soon with Squanto or Tisquantum, the only survivor of the Patuxet tribe of Indians which had perished of a pestilence Plymouth three years before. He shared with Hobomok the friendship of the settlers for many years and both Indians gave excellent service. Through the influence of Squanto the treaty was made in the spring of 1621 with Massasoit, the first League of Nations to preserve peace in the new world.

Squanto showed the men how to plant alewives or herring as fertilizer for the Indian corn. He taught the boys and girls how to gather clams and mussels on the shore and to "tread eels" in the water that is still called Eel River. He gathered wild strawberries and sassafras for the women and they prepared a "brew" which almost equalled their ale of old England. The friendly Indians assisted the men, as the seasons opened, in hunting wild turkeys, ducks and an occasional deer, welcome additions to the store of fish, sea-biscuits and cheese. We are told [Footnote: Mourt's Relation] that Squanto brought also a dog from his Indian friends as a gift to the settlement. Already there were, at least, two dogs, probably brought from Holland or England, a mastiff and a spaniel [Footnote: Winslow's Narration] to give comfort and companionship to the women and children, and to go with the men into the woods for timber and game.

It seems paradoxical to speak of child-life in this hard-pressed, serious-minded colony, but it was there and, doubtless, it was normal in its joyous and adventuresome impulses. Under eighteen years of age were the girls, Remember and Mary Allerton, Constance and Damaris Hopkins, Elizabeth Tilley and, possibly, Desire Minter and Humility Cooper. The boys were Bartholomew Allerton, who "learned to sound the drum," John Crakston, William Latham, Giles Hopkins, John and Francis Billington, Richard More, Henry Sampson, John Cooke, Resolved White, Samuel Fuller, Love and Wrestling Brewster and the babies, Oceanus Hopkins and Peregrine White. With the exception of Wrestling Brewster and Oceanus Hopkins, all these children lived to ripe old age,—a credit not alone to their hardy constitutions, but also to the care which the Plymouth women bestowed upon their households.

The flowers that grew in abundance about the settlement must have given them joy,—*arbutus* or "mayflowers," wild roses, blue chicory, Queen Anne's lace, purple asters, golden-rod and the beautiful sabbatia or "sentry" which is still found on the banks of the fresh ponds near the town and is called "the Plymouth rose." Edward Winslow tells [Footnote: Relation of the Manners, Customs, etc., of the Indians.] of the drastic use of this bitter plant in developing hardihood among Indian boys. Early in the first year one of these fresh-water ponds, known as Billington Sea, was discovered by Francis Billington when he had climbed a high hill and had reported from it "a smaller sea." Blackberries, blueberries, plums and cherries must have been delights to the women and children. Medicinal herbs were found and used by advice of the Indian friends; the bayberry's virtues as salve, if not as candle-light, were early applied to the comforts of the households. Robins, bluebirds, "Bob Whites" and other birds sang for the pioneers as they sing for the tourist and resident in Plymouth today. The mosquito had a sting,—for Bradford gave a droll and pungent answer to the discontented colonists who had reported, in 1624, that "the people are much annoyed with musquetoes." He wrote: [Footnote: Bradford's History of Plymouth Plantation, Bk. II.] "*They* are too delicate and unfitte to begin new plantations and colonies that cannot enduer the biting of a muskeet. We would wish such to keep at home till at least they be muskeeto proof. Yet this place is as free as any and experience teacheth that ye land is tild and ye woods cut downe, the fewer there will be and in the end scarce any at all." The *end* has not yet come!

Good harvests and some thrilling incidents varied the hard conditions of life for the women during 1621-2. Indian corn and barley furnished a new foundation for many "a savory dish" prepared by the housewives in the mortar and pestles, kettles and skillets which they had brought from Holland. Nuts were used for food, giving piquant flavor both to "cakes" baked in the fire and to the stuffing of wild turkeys. The fare was simple, but it must have seemed a feast to the Pilgrims after the months of self-denials and extremity.

Before the winter of 1621-2 was ended, seven log houses had been built and four "common buildings" for storage, meetings and workshops. Already clapboards and furs were stored to be sent back to England to the merchant adventurers in the first ship. The seven huts, with thatched roofs and chimneys on the outside, probably in cob-house style, were of hewn planks, not of round logs. [Footnote: The Pilgrim Republic, John A. Goodwin, p. 582.] The fireplaces were of stones laid in clay from the abundant sand. In 1628 thatched roofs were condemned because of the danger of fire, [Footnote: Records of the Colony of New Plymouth.] and boards or palings were substituted. During the first two years or longer, light came into the houses through oiled paper in the windows. From the plans left by Governor Bradford and the record of the visit of De Rassieres to Plymouth, in 1627, one can visualize this first street in New England, leading from Plymouth harbor up the hill to the cannon and stockade where, later, was the fort. At the intersection of the first street and a cross-highway stood the Governor's house. It was fitting that the lot nearest to the fort hill should be assigned to Miles Standish and John Alden. All had free access to the brook where flagons were filled for drink and where the clothes were washed.

A few events that have been recorded by Winslow, Bradford and Morton were significant and must have relieved the monotony of life. On January fourth an eagle was shot, cooked and proved "to be excellent meat; it was hardly to be discerned from mutton." [Footnote: Mourt's Relation.] Four days later three seals and a cod were caught; we may assume that they furnished oil, meat and skins for the household. About the same time, John Goodman and Peter Brown lost their way in the woods, remained out all night, thinking they heard lions roar (mistaking wolves for lions), and on their return the next day John Goodman's feet were so badly frozen "that it was a long time before he was able to go." [Footnote: Ibid.] Wild geese were shot and used for broth on the ninth of February; the same day the Common House was set ablaze, but was saved from destruction. It is easy to imagine the exciting effects of such incidents upon the band of thirteen boys and seven girls, already enumerated. In July, the cry of "a lost child" aroused the settlement to a search for that "unwhipt rascal," John Billington, who had run away to the Nauset Indians at Eastham, but he was found unharmed by a posse of men led by Captain Standish.

To the women one of the most exciting events must have been the marriage on May 22, 1621, of Edward Winslow and Mistress Susanna White. Her husband and two men-servants had died since *The Mayflower* left England and she was alone to care for two young boys, one a baby a few weeks old. Elizabeth Barker Winslow had died seven weeks before the wedding day. Perhaps the Plymouth women gossiped a little over the brief interval of mourning, but the exigencies of the times easily explained the marriage, which was performed by a magistrate, presumably the Governor.

Even more disturbing to the peaceful life was the first duel on June 18, between Edward Lister and Edward Dotey, both servants of Stephen Hopkins. Tradition ascribed the cause to a quarrel over the attractive elder daughter of their master, Constance Hopkins. The duel was fought with swords and daggers; both youths were slightly wounded in hand and thigh and both were sentenced, as punishment, to have their hands and feet tied together and to fast for twenty-four hours but, says a record, [Footnote: A Chronological History of New England, by Thomas Prence.] "within an hour, because of their great pains, at their own and their master's humble request, upon promise of better carriage, they were released by the Governor." It is easy to imagine this scene: Stephen Hopkins and his wife appealing to the Governor and Captain Standish for leniency, although the settlement was seriously troubled over the occurrence; Elder Brewster and his wife deploring the lack of Christian affection which caused the duel; Edward Winslow and his wife, dignified yet tolerant; Goodwife Helen Billington scolding as usual; Priscilla Mullins, Mary Chilton and Elizabeth Tilley condoling with the tearful and frightened Constance Hopkins, while the children stand about, excited and somewhat awed by the punishment and the distress of the offenders.

Another day of unusual interest and industry for the householders was the Thanksgiving Day when peace with the Indians and assured prosperity seemed to follow the ample harvests. To this feast, which lasted for three days or more, came ninety-one Indians bringing five deer which they had killed and dressed. These were a great boon to the women who must prepare meals for one hundred and forty people. Wild turkeys, ducks, fish and clams were procured by the colonists and cooked, perhaps with some marchpanes also, by the more expert cooks. The serious prayers and psalms of the Pilgrims were as amazing to the Indians as were the strange whoops, dances, beads and feathers of the savages marvellous to the women and children of Plymouth Colony.

In spite of these peaceable incidents there were occasional threats of Indian treachery, like the theft of tools from two woodsmen and the later bold challenge in the form of a headless arrow wrapped in a snake's skin; the latter was returned promptly and decisively with the skin filled with bullets, and the danger was over for a time. The stockade was strengthened and, soon after, a palisade was built about the houses with gates that were locked at night. After the fort of heavy timber was completed, this was used also as a meeting-house and "was fitted accordingly for that use." It is to be hoped that warming-pans and foot-stoves were a part of the "fittings" so that the women might not be benumbed as, with dread of possible Indian attacks, they limned from the old Ainsworth's Psalm Book:

> *"In the Lord do I trust, how then to my soule doe ye say,*
> *As doth a little bird unto your mountaine fly away?*
> *For loe, the wicked bend their bow, their arrows they prepare*
> *On string; to shoot at dark at them*
> *In heart that upright are."*
> *(Psalm xi.)*

Even more exciting than the days already mentioned was the great event of surprise and rejoicing, November 19, 1621, when *The Fortune* arrived with thirty-five more Pilgrims. Some of these were soon to wed *Mayflower* passengers. Widow Martha Ford, recently bereft, giving birth on the night of her arrival to a fourth child, was wed to Peter Brown; Mary Becket (sometimes written Bucket) became the wife of George Soule; John Winslow; later married Mary Chilton, and Thomas Cushman, then a lad of fourteen, became the husband, in manhood, of Mary Allerton. His father, Robert Cushman, remained in the settlement while *The Fortune* was at anchor and left his son as ward for Governor Bradford. The notable sermon which was preached at Plymouth by Robert Cushman at this time (preserved in Pilgrim Hall, Plymouth) was from the text, "Let no man seek his own; but every man another's wealth." Some of the admonitions against swelling pride and fleshly-minded hypocrites seem to us rather paradoxical when we consider the poverty and self-sacrificing spirit of these pioneers; perhaps, there were selfish and slothful malcontents even in that company of devoted, industrious men and women, for human nature was the same three hundred years ago, in large and small communities, as it is today, with some relative changes.

Among the passengers brought by *The Fortune* were some of great helpfulness. William Wright, with his wife Priscilla (the sister of Governor Bradford's second wife), was an expert carpenter, and Stephen Dean, who came with his wife, was able to erect a small mill and grind corn. Robert Hicks (or Heeks) was another addition to the colony, whose wife was later the teacher of some of the children. Philip De La Noye, progenitor of the Delano family in America, John and Kenelm Winslow and Jonathan Brewster were eligible men to join the group of younger men,—John Alden, John Howland and others.

The great joy in the arrival of these friends was succeeded by an agitating fear regarding the food supply, for *The Fortune* had suffered from bad weather and its colonists had scarcely any extra food or clothing. By careful allotments the winter was endured and when spring came there were hopes of a large harvest from more abundant sowing, but the hopes were killed by the fearful drought which lasted from May to the middle of July. Some lawless and selfish youths frequently stole corn before it was ripe and, although public whipping was the punishment, the evil persisted. These conditions were met with the same courage and determination which ever characterized the leaders; a rationing of the colony was made which would have done credit to a "Hoover." They escaped famine, but the worn, thin faces and "the low condition, both in respect of food and clothing" was a shock to the sixty more colonists who arrived in *The Ann* and *The James* in 1623.

The friends who came in these later ships included some women from Leyden, "dear gossips" of *Mayflower* colonists, women whose resources and characters gave them prominence in the later history of Plymouth. Notable among them was Mrs. Alice Southworth soon to wed Governor Bradford. With her came Barbara, whose surname is surmised to have been Standish, soon to become the wife of Captain Standish. Bridget Fuller joined her husband, the noble doctor of Plymouth; Elizabeth Warren, with her five daughters, came to make a home for her husband, Richard; Mistress Hester Cooke came with three children, and Fear and Patience Brewster, despite their names, brought joy and cheer to their mother and girlhood friends; they were later wed to Isaac Allerton and Thomas Prence, the Governor.

Fortunately, *The Ann* and *The James* brought supplies in liberal measure and also carpenters, weavers and cobblers, for their need was great. *The James* was to remain for the use of the colony. Rations had been as low as one-quarter pound of bread a day and sometimes their fare was only "a bit of fish or lobster without any bread or relish but a cup of fair spring water." [Footnote: Bradford's History of Plymouth Plantation; Bk. II.] It is not strange that Bradford added: "ye long continuance of this diete and their labors abroad had somewhat abated ye freshness of their former complexion."

An important change in the policy of the colony, which affected the women as well as men, was made at this time. Formerly the administration of affairs had been upon the communal basis. All the men and grown boys were expected to plant and harvest, fish and hunt for the common use of all the households. The women also did their tasks in common. The results had been unsatisfactory and, in 1623, a new division of land was made, allotting to member householder an acre for each member of his family. This arrangement, which was called "every man for his owne particuler," was told by Bradford with a comment which shows that the women were human beings, not saints nor martyrs. He wrote: "The women now went willingly into ye field, and tooke their little-ones with them to set corne, which before would aledge weaknes and inabilitie; whom to have compelled would have bene thought great tiranie and oppression." After further comment upon the failure of communism as "breeding confusion and discontent" he added this significant comment: "For ye yong-men that were most able and fitte for labour and service did repine that they should spend their time and strength to work for other men's wives and children without any recompense.... And for men's wives to be commanded to doe servise for other men, as dresing their meate, washing their cloathes, etc., they deemed it a kind of slaverie, neither could many husbands well brooke it."

If food was scarce, even a worse condition existed as to clothing in the summer of 1623. Tradition has ascribed several spinning-wheels and looms to the women who came in *The Mayflower*, but we can scarcely believe that such comforts were generously bestowed. There could have been little material or time for their use. Much skilful weaving and spinning of linen, flax, and wool came in later Colonial history. The women must have been taxed to keep the clothes mended for their families as protection against the cold and storms. The quantity on hand, after the stress of the two years, would vary according to the supplies which each brought from Holland or England; in some families there were sheets and "pillow-beeres" with "clothes of substance and comeliness," but other households were scantily supplied. A somewhat crude but interesting ballad, called "Our Forefathers' Song," is given by tradition from the lips of an old lady aged ninety-four years, in 1767. If the suggestion is accurate that she learned this from her mother or grandmother, its date would approximate the early days of Plymouth history. More probably it was written much later, but it has a reminiscent flavor of those days of poverty and brave spirit:

"The place where we live is a wilderness wood,

Where grass is much wanted that's fruitful and good;

Our mountains and hills and our valleys below,
Are commonly covered with frost and with snow.

"Our clothes we brought with us are apt to be torn,
They need to be clouted soon after they are worn,
But clouting our garments they hinder us nothing,
Clouts double are warmer than single whole clothing.

"If fresh meate be wanted to fill up our dish,
We have carrots and turnips whenever we wish,
And if we've a mind for a delicate dish,
We go to the clam-bank and there we catch fish.

"For pottage and puddings and custards and pies,
Our pumpkins and parsnips are common supplies!
We have pumpkin at morning and pumpkin at noon,
If it was not for pumpkin we should be undoon."

[Footnote: The Pilgrim Fathers; W. H. Bartlett, London, 1852.]

What did these Pilgrim women wear? The manifest answer is,—what they had in stock. No more absurd idea was ever invented than the picture of these Pilgrims "in uniform," gray gowns with dainty white collars and cuffs, with stiff caps and dark capes. They wore the typical garments of the period for men and women in England. There is no evidence that they adopted, to any extent, Dutch dress, for they were proud of their English birth; they left Holland partly for fear that their young people might be educated or enticed away from English standards of conduct. [Footnote: Bradford's History of Plymouth Plantation, ch. 4.] Mrs. Alice Morse Earle has emphasized wisely [Footnote: Two Centuries of Costume in America; N. Y., 1903.] that the "sad-colored" gowns and coats mentioned in wills were not "dismal"; the list of colors so described in England included (1638) "russet, purple, green, tawny, deere colour, orange colour, buffs and scarlet." The men wore doublets and jerkins of browns and greens, and cloaks with red and purple linings. The women wore full skirts of say, paduasoy or silk of varied colors, long, pointed stomachers,—often with bright tone,—full, sometimes puffed or slashed sleeves, and lace collars or "whisks" resting upon the shoulders. Sometimes the gowns were plaited or silk-laced; they often opened in front showing petticoats that were quilted or embroidered in brighter colours. Broadcloth gowns of russet tones were worn by those who could not afford silks and satins; sometimes women wore doublets and jerkins of black and browns. For dress occasions the men wore black velvet jerkins with white ruffs, like those in the authentic portrait of Edward Winslow. Velvet and quilted hoods of all colors and sometimes caps, flat on the head and meeting below the chin with fullness, are shown in existent portraits of English women and early colonists.

Among relics that are dated back to this early period are the slipper [Footnote: In Pilgrim Hall, Plymouth.] belonging to Mistress Susanna White Winslow, narrow, pointed, with lace trimmings, and an embroidered lace cap that has been assigned to Rose Standish. [Footnote: Two Centuries of Costume In America; Earle.] Sometimes the high ruffs were worn above the shoulders instead of "whisks." The children were dressed like miniature men and women; often the girls wore aprons, as did the women on occasions; these were narrow and edged with lace. "Petty coats" are mentioned in wills among the garments of the women. We would not assume that in 1621-2 *all* the women in Plymouth colony wore silken or even homespun clothes of prevailing English fashion. Many of these that are mentioned in inventories and retained heirlooms, with rich laces and embroideries, were brought later from England; probably Winslow, Allerton and even Standish brought back such gifts to the women when they made their trips to England in 1624 and later. If the pioneer women had laces and embroideries of gold they probably hoarded them as precious heirlooms during those early years of want, for they were too sensible to wear and to waste them. As prosperity came, however, and new elements entered the colony they were, doubtless, affected by the law of the General Court, in 1634, which forbade further acquisition of laces, threads of silver and gold, needle-work caps, bands and rails, and silver girdles and belts. This law was enacted *not* by the Pilgrims of Plymouth, but by the Puritans of Massachusetts Bay Colony.

When Edward Winslow returned in *The Charity*, in 1624, he brought not alone a "goodly supply of clothing" [Footnote: Bradford's History of Plymouth Plantation, Bk. 2.] but,—far more important,—the first bull and heifers that were in Plymouth. The old tradition of the white bull on which Priscilla Alden rode home from her marriage, in 1622 or early 1623, must be rejected. This valuable addition of "neat cattle" to the resources of the colony caused a redistribution of land and shares in the "stock." By 1627 a partnership or "purchas" had been, arranged, for assuming the debts and maintenance of the Plymouth colony, freed from further responsibility to "the adventurers" in London. The new division of lots included also some of the cattle. It was specified, for instance, that Captain Standish and Edward Winslow were to share jointly "the Red Cow which belongeth to the poor of the colony to which they must keep her Calfe of this yeare being a Bull for the Companie, Also two shee goats." [Footnote: Records of the Colony of New Plymouth In New England, edited by David Pulslfer, 1861.] Elder Brewster was granted "one of the four Heifers came in *The Jacob* called the Blind Heifer."

Among interesting sidelights upon the economic and social results of this extension of land and cattle is the remark of Bradford: [Footnote: Bradford's History of Plymouth Plantation, Bk. 2.] "Some looked for building great houses, and such pleasant situations for them as themselves had fancied, as if they would be great men and rich all of a suddaine; but they proved castles in air." Within a short time, however, with the rapid increase of children and the need of more pasturage for the cattle, many of the leading men and women drifted away from the original confines of Plymouth towards Duxbury, Marshfield, Scituate, Bridgewater and Eastham. Agriculture became their primal concern, with the allied pursuits of fishing, hunting and trading with the Indians and white settlements that were made on Cape Cod and along the Kennebec.

Soon after 1630 the families of Captain Standish, John Alden, and Jonathan Brewster (who had married the sister of John Oldham), Thomas Prence and Edward Winslow were settled on large farms in Duxbury and Marshfield. This loss to the Plymouth settlement was deplored by Bradford both for its social and religious results. April 2, 1632, [Footnote: Records of the Colony of New Plymouth In New England, edited by David Pulslfer, 1861.] a pledge was taken by Alden, Standish, Prence, and Jonathan Brewster that they would "remove their families to live in the towne in the winter-time that they may the better repair to the service of God." Such arrangement did not long continue, however, for in 1633 a church was established at Duxbury and the Plymouth members who lived there "were dismiste though very unwillingly." [Footnote: Bradford's History of Plymouth Plantation, Bk. 2.] Later the families of Francis Eaton, Peter Brown and George Soule joined the Duxbury colony. Hobomok, ever faithful to Captain Standish had a wigwam near his master's home until, in his old age, he was removed to the Standish house, where he died in 1642.

The women who had come in the earlier ships and had lived close to neighbors at Plymouth must have had lonely hours on their farms in spite of large families and many tasks. Wolves and other wild animals were sometimes near, for traps for them were decreed and allotted. Chance Indians prowled about and the stoutest hearts must have quailed when some of the recorded hurricanes and storms of 1635 and 1638 uncovered houses, felled trees and corn. In the main, however, there was peace and many of the families became prosperous; we find evidence in their wills, several of which have been deciphered from the original records by George Ernest Bowman, editor of the "Mayflower Descendants," [Footnote: Editorial rooms at 53 Mt. Vernon St., Boston.] issued quarterly. By the aid of such records and a few family heirlooms of unquestioned genuineness, it is possible to suggest some individual silhouettes of the women of early Plymouth, in addition to the glimpses of their communal life.

CHAPTER III
MATRONS AND MAIDENS WHO CAME IN THE MAYFLOWER

It has been said, with some justice, that the Pilgrims were not remarkable men, that they lacked genius or distinctive personalities. The same statement may be made about the women. They did possess, as men and women, fine qualities for the work which they were destined to accomplish,—remarkable energy, faith, purpose, courage and patience. These traits were prominent in the leaders, Carver and Bradford, Standish and Winslow, Brewster and Dr. Fuller. As assistants to the men in the civic life of the colony, there were a few women who influenced the domestic and social affairs of their own and later generations. From chance records, wills, inventories and traditions their individual traits must be discerned, for there is scarcely any sequential, historic record.

Death claimed some of these brave-hearted women before the life at Plymouth really began. Dorothy May Bradford, the daughter of Deacon May of the Leyden church, came from Wisbeach, Cambridge; she was married to William Bradford when she was about sixteen years old and was only twenty when she was drowned at Cape Cod. Her only child, a son, John, was left with her father and mother in Holland and there was long a tradition that she mourned grievously at the separation. This son came later to Plymouth, about 1627, and lived in Marshfield and Norwich, Connecticut.

The tiny pieces of a padded quilt with faded threads of silver and gold, which belonged to Rose Standish, [Footnote: Now in Pilgrim Hall, Plymouth.] are fitting relics of this mystical, delicate wife of "the doughty Captain." She died January 29, 1621. She is portrayed in fiction and poetry as proud of her husband's bravery and his record as a Lieutenant of Queen Elizabeth's forces in aid of the Dutch. She was also proud of his reputed, and disputed, inheritance among the titled families of Standish of Standish and Standish of Duxbury Hall. [Footnote: For discussion of the ancestry of

Standish, see "Some Recent Investigations of the Ancestry of Capt. Myles Standish," by Thomas Cruddas Porteus of Coppell, Lancashire; N. E. Gen. Hist. Register, 68; 339-370; also in edition, Boston, 1914.] There has been a persistent tradition that Rose was born or lived on the Isle of Man and was married there, but no records have been found as proofs.

In the painting of "The Embarkation," by Robert Weir, Elizabeth Barker, the young wife of Edward Winslow, is attired in gay colors and extreme fashion, while beside her stands a boy of about eight years with a canteen strapped over his shoulders. It has been stated that this is the silver canteen, marked "E. W.," now in the cabinet of the Massachusetts Historical Society. The only record *there* is [Footnote: Massachusetts Historical Society Proceedings, iv, 322.] "presentation, June, 1870, by James Warren, Senr., of a silver canteen and pewter plate which once belonged to Gov. Edward Winslow with his arms and initials." As Elizabeth Barker, who came from Chatsun or Chester, England, to Holland, was married April 3, 1618, to Winslow, [Footnote: England and Holland of the Pilgrims, Dexter.] and as she was his first wife, the son must have been a baby when *The Mayflower* sailed. Moreover, there is no record by Bradford of any child that came with the Winslows, except the orphan, Ellen More. It has been suggested that the latter was of noble lineage. [Footnote: The Mayflower Descendant, v. 256.]

Mary Norris, of Newbury in England, wife of one of the wealthiest and most prominent of the Pilgrims in early years, Isaac Allerton, died in February of the first winter, leaving two young girls, Remember and Mary, and a son, Bartholomew or "Bart." The daughters married well, Remember to Moses Maverick of Salem, and Mary to Thomas Cushman. Mrs. Allerton gave birth to a child that was still-born while on *The Mayflower* and thus she had less strength to endure the hardships which followed. [Footnote: History of the Allerton Family; W. S. Allerton, N. Y., 1888.]

When Bradford, recording the death of Katherine Carver, called her a "weak woman," he referred to her health which was delicate while she lived at Plymouth and could not withstand the grief and shock of her husband's death in April. She died the next month. She has been called "a gracious woman" in another record of her death. [Footnote: New England Memorial; Morton.] She was the sister or sister-in-law of John Robinson, their pastor in England and Holland. Recent investigation has claimed that she was first married to George Legatt and later to Carver. [Footnote: The Colonial, I, 46; also Gen. Hist. Reg., 67; 382, note.] Two children died and were buried in Holland in 1609 and 1617 and, apparently, these were the only children born to the Carvers. The maid Lois, who came with them on *The Mayflower*, is supposed to have married Francis Eaton, but she did not live after 1622. Desire Minter, who was also of the Carver household, has been the victim of much speculation. Mrs. Jane G. Austin, in her novel, "Standish of Standish," makes her the female scapegrace of the colony, jealous, discontented and quarrelsome. On the other hand, and still speculatively, she is portrayed as the elder sister and house keeper for John Howland and Elizabeth Tilley, after the death of Mistress Carver; this is assumed because the first girl born to the Howlands was named Desire. [Footnote: Life of Pilgrim Alden; Augustus E. Alden; Boston, 1902.] The only known facts about Desire Minter are those given by Bradford, "she returned to friends and proved not well, and dyed in England." [Footnote: Bradford's History of Plymouth Plantation; Appendix.] By research among the Leyden records, collated by H. M. Dexter, [Footnote: The England and Holland of the Pilgrims.] the name, Minter, occurs a few times. William Minter, the husband of Sarah, was associated with the Carvers and Chiltons in marriage betrothals. William Minter was purchaser of a house from William Jeppson, in Leyden, in 1614. Another record is of a student at the University of Leyden who lived at the house of John Minter. Another reference to Thomas Minter of Sandwich, Kent, may furnish a clue. [Footnote: N. E. Gen. Hist. Reg., 45, 56.] Evidently, to some of these relatives, with property, near or distant of kin, Desire Minter returned before 1626.

Another unmarried woman, who survived the hardships of the first winter, but returned to England and died there, was Humility Cooper. We know almost nothing about her except that she and Henry Sampson were cousins of Edward Tilley and his wife. She is also mentioned as a relative of Richard Clopton, one of the early religious leaders in England. [Footnote: N. E. Gen. Hist.; iv, 108.]

The "mother" of this group of matrons and maidens, who survived the winters of 1621-2, was undoubtedly Mistress Mary Brewster. Wife of the Elder, she shared his religious faith and zeal, and exercised a strong moral influence upon the women and children. Pastor John Robinson, in a letter to Governor Bradford, in 1623, refers to "her weake and decayed state of body," but she lived until April 17, 1627, according to records in "the Brewster Book." She was only fifty-seven years at her death but, as Bradford said with tender appreciation, "her great and continuall labours, with other crosses and sorrows, hastened it before y'e time." As Elder Brewster "could fight as well as he could pray," could build his own house and till his own land, [Footnote: The Pilgrim Republic; John A. Goodwin.] so, we may believe, his wife was efficient in all domestic ways. When her strength failed, it is pleasant to think that she accepted graciously the loving assistance of the younger women to whom she must have seemed, in her presence, like a benediction. Her married life was fruitful; five children lived to maturity and two or more had died in Holland. The Elder was "wise and discreet and well-spoken—of a cheerful spirit, sociable and pleasant among his friends, undervaluing himself and his abilities and sometimes overvaluing others." [Footnote: Bradford's History of Plymouth Plantation.] Such a person is sure to be a delightful companion. To these attractive qualities the Elder added another proof of tact and wisdom: "He always thought it were better for ministers to pray oftener and divide their prayers, than be long and tedious in the same."

While Mistress Brewster did not excel the women of her day, probably, in education, for to read easily and to write were not considered necessary graces for even the better-bred classes,—she could appreciate the thirty-eight copies of the Scriptures which were found among her husband's four hundred volumes; *these* would be familiar to her, but the sixty-four books in Latin would not be read by the women of her day. Fortunately, she did not survive, as did her husband, to endure grief from the deaths of the daughters, Fear and Patience, both of whom died before 1635; nor yet did she realize the bitterness of feeling between the sons, Jonathan and Love, and their differences of opinion in the settlement of the Elder's estate. [Footnote: Records of the Colony of New Plymouth.]

A traditional picture has been given [Footnote: The Pilgrim Republic; John A. Goodwin; foot-note, p.181.] of Captain Peregrine White of Marshfield, "riding a black horse and wearing a coat with buttons the size of a silver dollar, vigorous and of a comely aspect to the last," [Footnote: Account of his death in *Boston News Letter*, July 31, 1704.] paying daily visits to his mother, Mistress Susanna White Winslow. We may imagine this elderly matron, sitting in the Winslow arm-chair, with its mark, "Cheapside, 1614," [Footnote: This chair and the cape are now In Pilgrim Hall, Plymouth; here also are portraits of Edward Winslow and Josiah Winslow and the latter's wife, Penelope.] perhaps wearing the white silk shoulder-cape with its trimmings of embossed velvet which has been preserved, proud that she was privileged to be the mother of this son, the first child born of white parents in New England, proud that she had been the wife of a Governor and Commissioner of eminence, and also the mother of Josiah Winslow, the first native-born Governor of any North American commonwealth. Hers was a record of which any woman of any century might well be proud! [Footnote: More material may be found in Winslow Memorial; Family Record, Holton, N. Y., 1877, and in Ancestral Chronological Record of the William White Family, 1607-1895, Concord, 1895.]

In social position and worldly comforts her life was pre-eminent among the colonists. Although Edward Winslow had renounced some of his English wealth, possibly, when he went to Holland and adopted the trade of printer, he "came into his own" again and was in high favor with English courts and statesmen. His services as agent and commissioner, both for the Plymouth colony and later for Cromwell, must have necessitated long absences from home, while his wife remained at Careswell, the estate at Green Harbor, Marshfield, caring for her younger children, Elizabeth and Josiah Winslow. By family tradition, Mistress Susanna was a woman of graceful, aristocratic bearing and of strong character. Sometimes called Anna, as in her marriage record to William White at Leyden, February 11, 1612, [Footnote: The Mayflower Descendant, vii, 193.] she was the sister of Dr. Samuel Fuller. Two children by her first marriage died in 1615 and 1616; with her boy, Resolved, about five or six years old, she came with her husband on *The Mayflower* and, at the end of the voyage, bore her son, Peregrine White.

The tact, courtesy and practical sagacity of Edward Winslow fitted him for the many demands that were made upon his diplomacy. One of the most amusing stories of his experiences as agent for Plymouth colony has been related by himself [Footnote: Winslow's Relation.] when, at the request of the Indians, he visited Massasoit, who was ill, and brought about the recovery of this chief by common sense methods of treatment and by a "savory broth" made from Indian corn, sassafras and strawberry leaves, "strained through his handkerchief." The skill with which Winslow cooked the broth and the "relish" of ducks reflected credit upon the household methods of Mistress Winslow.

After 1646, Edward Winslow did not return to Plymouth for any long sojourn, for Cromwell and his advisers had recognized the worth of such a man as commissioner. [Footnote: State Papers, Colonial Service, 1574-1660. Winthrop Papers, ii, 283.] In 1655 he was sent as one of three commissioners against the Spaniards in the West Indies to attack St. Domingo. Because of lack of supplies and harmony among the troops, the attack was a failure. To atone for this the fleet started towards Jamaica, but on the way, near

Hispaniola, Winslow was taken ill of fever and died, May 8, 1655; he was buried at sea with a military salute from forty-two guns. The salary paid to Winslow during these years was £1000, which was large for those times. On April 18, 1656, a "representation" from his widow, Susanna, and son was presented to the Lord Protector and council, asking that, although Winslow's death occurred the previous May, the remaining £500 of his year's salary might be paid to satisfy his creditors.

To his wife and family Winslow, doubtless, wrote letters as graceful and interesting as are the few business epistles that are preserved in the Winthrop Papers. [Footnote: Hutchinson Collections, 110, 153, etc.] That he was anxious, to return to his family is evident from a letter by President Steele of the Society for Propagating the Gospel in New England (in 1650), which Winslow was also serving; [Footnote: The Pilgrim Republic; Goodwin, 444.] "Winslow was unwilling to be longer kept from his family, but his great acquaintance and influence were of service to the cause so great that it was hoped he would remain for a time longer." In his will, which is now in Somerset House, London, dated 1654, he left his estate at Marshfield to his son, Josiah, with the stipulation that his wife, Susanna, should be allowed a full third part thereof through her life. [Footnote: The Mayflower Descendant, iv. i.] She lived twenty-five years longer, dying in October, 1680, at the estate, Careswell. It is supposed that she was buried on the hillside cemetery of the Daniel Webster estate in Marshfield, where, amid tangles and flowers, may be located the grave-stones of her children and grandchildren. Sharing with Mistress Susanna White Winslow the distinction of being mother of a child born on *The Mayflower* was Mistress Elizabeth Hopkins, whose son, Oceanus, was named for his birthplace. She was the second wife of Stephen Hopkins, who was one of the leaders with Winslow and Standish on early expeditions. With her stepchildren, Constance and Giles, and her little daughter, Damaris, she bore the rigors of those first years, bore other children,—Caleb, Ruth, Deborah and Elizabeth,—and cared for a large estate, including servants and many cattle. The inventory of the Hopkins estate revealed an abundance of beds and bedding, yellow and green rugs, curtains and spinning-wheels, and much wearing apparel. The home-life surely had incidents of excitement, as is shown by the accusations and fines against Stephen Hopkins for "suffering excessive drinking at his house, 1637, when William Reynolds was drunk and lay under the table," and again for "suffering men to drink in his house on the Lord's Day, both before and after the meeting—and allowing his servant and others to drink more than for ordinary refreshing and to play shovell board and such like misdemeanors." [Footnote: Records of the Colony of New Plymouth.] Such lapses in conduct at the Hopkins house were atoned for by the services which Stephen Hopkins rendered to the colony as explorer, assistant to the governor and other offices which suited his reliable and fearless disposition.

These occasional "misdemeanors" in the Hopkins household were slight compared with the records against "the black sheep" of the colony, the family of Billingtons from London. The mother, Helen or Ellen, did not seem to redeem the reputation of husband and sons; traditionally she was called "the scold." After her husband had been executed in 1630, for the first murder in the colony, for he had waylaid and killed John Newcomen, she married Gregory Armstrong. She had various controversies in court with her son and others. In 1636, she was accused of slander by "Deacon" John Doane,—she had charged him with unfairness in mowing her pasture lot,—and she was sentenced to a fine of five pounds and "to sit in the stocks and be publickly whipt." [Footnote: Records of the Colony of New Plymouth.] Her second husband died in 1650 and she lived several years longer, occupying a "tenement" granted to her in her son's house at North Plymouth. Apparently her son, John, after his fractious youth, died; Francis married Christian Penn, the widow of Francis Eaton.

Their children seem to have "been bound out" for service while the parents were convicted of trying to entice the children away from their work and, consequently, they were punished by sitting in the stocks on "lecture days." [Footnote: The Pilgrim Republic; Goodwin.] In his later life, Francis Billington became more stable in character and served on committees. His last offense was the mild one "of drinking tobacco on the high-way." Apparently, Helen Billington had many troubles and little sympathy in the Plymouth colony.

As companions to these matrons of the pioneer days were four maidens who must have been valuable as assistants in housework and care of the children,—Priscilla Mullins, Mary Chilton, Elizabeth Tilley and Constance Hopkins. The first three had been orphaned during that first winter; probably, they became members of the households of Elder Brewster and Governor Carver. All have left names that are most honorably cherished by their many descendants. Priscilla Mullins has been celebrated in romance and poetry. Very little real knowledge exists about her and many of the surmises would be more interesting if they could be proved. She was well-born, for her father, at his death, was mentioned with regret [Footnote: New England Memorial; Morton.] as "a man pious and well-deserving, endowed also with considerable outward estate; and had it been the will of God, that he had survived, might have proved an useful instrument in his place." There was a family tradition of a castle, Molyneux or Molines, in Normandy. The title of *Mr.* indicated that he was a man of standing and he was a counsellor in state and church. Perhaps he died on shipboard at Plymouth, because his, will, dated April 2, 1621, was witnessed by John Carver, Christopher Jones and Giles Heald, probably the captain and surgeon of the ship, *Mayflower.*

This will, which has been recently found in Dorking, Surrey, England, has had important influence upon research. We learn that an older sister, Sarah Blunden, living in Surrey, was named as administratrix, and that a son, William (who came to Plymouth before 1637) was to have money, bonds and stocks in England. Goods in Virginia and more money,—ten pounds each,—were bequeathed equally to his wife Alice, his daughter Priscilla and the younger son, Joseph. Interesting also is the item of "xxj dozen shoes and thirteene paire of boots wch I give unto the Companie's hands for forty pounds at seaven yeares." If the Company would not accept the rate, these shoes and boots were to be for the equal benefit of his wife and son, William. To his friend, John Carver, he commits his wife and children and also asks for a "special eye to my man Robert wch hath not so approved himself as I would he should have done." [Footnote: Pilgrim Alden, by Augustus E. Alden, Boston, 1902.] Before this will was probated, July 23, 1621, John Carver, Mistress Alice Mullins, the son, Joseph, and the man, Robert Carter (or Cartier) were all dead, leaving Priscilla to carry on the work to which they had pledged their lives. Perhaps, the brother and sister in England were children of an earlier marriage, [Footnote: Gen. Hist. Register, 40; 62-3.] as Alice Mullins has been spoken of as a second wife.

Priscilla was about twenty years old when she came to Plymouth. By tradition she was handsome, witty, deft and skilful as spinner and cook. Into her life came John Alden, a cooper of unknown family, who joined the Pilgrims at Southampton, under promise to stay a year. Probably he was not the first suitor for Priscilla's hand, for tradition affirmed that she had been sought in Leyden. The single sentence by Bradford tells the story of their romance: "being a hop[e]full yong man was much desired, but left to his owne liking to go or stay when he came here; but he stayed, and maryed here." With him he brought a Bible, printed 1620, [Footnote: Now in Pilgrim Hall, Plymouth.] probably a farewell gift or purchase as he left England.

When the grant of land and cattle was made in 1627, he was twenty-eight years old, and had in his family, Priscilla, his wife, a daughter, Elizabeth, aged three, and a son, John, aged one. [Footnote: Records of the Colony of New Plymouth.]

The poet, Longfellow, was a descendant of Priscilla Alden, and he had often heard the story of the courtship of Priscilla by Miles Standish, through John Alden as his proxy. It was said to date back to a poem, "Courtship," by Moses Mullins, 1672. In detail it was given by Timothy Alden in "American Epitaphs," 1814, [Footnote: American Epitaphs, 1814; iii, 139.] but there are here some deflections from facts as later research has revealed them. The magic words of romance, "Why don't you speak for yourself, John?" are found in this early narrative.

There was more than romance in the lives of John and Priscilla Alden as the "vital facts" indicate. Their first home was at Town Square, Plymouth, on the site of the first school-house but, by 1633, they lived upon a farm of one hundred and sixty-nine acres in Duxbury. Their first house here was about three hundred feet from the present Alden house, which was built by the son, Jonathan, and is now occupied by the eighth John Alden. It must have been a lonely farmstead for Priscilla, although she made rare visits, doubtless on an ox or a mare, or in an ox-cart with her children, to see Barbara Standish at Captain's Hill, or to the home of Jonathan Brewster, a few miles distant. As farmer, John Alden was not so successful as he would have been at his trade of cooper. Moreover, he gave much of his time to the service of the colony throughout his manhood, acting as assistant to the Governor, treasurer, surveyor, agent and military recruit. Like many another public servant of his day and later, he "became low in his estate" and was allowed a small gratuity of ten pounds because "he hath been occationed to spend time at the Courts on the Countryes occasion and soe hath done this many yeares." [Footnote: Records of the Colony of New Plymouth.] He had also been one of the eight "undertakers" who, in 1627, assumed the debts and financial support of the Plymouth colony.

Eleven children had been born to John and Priscilla Alden, five sons and six daughters. Sarah married Alexander Standish and so cemented the two families in blood as well as in friendship. Ruth, who married John Bass, became the ancestress of John Adams and John Quincy Adams. Elizabeth, who married William Pabodie, had thirteen children, eleven of them girls, and lived to be ninety-three years; at her death the *Boston News Letter* [Footnote: June 17, 1717.] extolled her as "exemplary, virtuous and pious and her memory is blessed." Possibly with all her piety she had a good share of the independence of spirit which was accredited to her mother; in her husband's will [Footnote: The Mayflower Descendant, vi, 129.] she is given her "third at Little Compton" and an abundance of household stuff, but with this reservation,—"If she will not be contented with her thirds at Little Compton, but shall claim her thirds in both Compton and Duxbury or marry again, I do hereby make voyde all my bequest unto her and she shall share only the parte as if her husband died intestate." A portrait of her shows dress of rich materials.

Captain John Alden seems to have been more adventuresome than the other boys in Priscilla's family. He was master of a merchantman in Boston and commander of armed vessels which supplied marine posts with provisions. Like his sister, Elizabeth, he had thirteen children. He was once accused of witchcraft, when he was present at a trial, and was imprisoned fifteen weeks without being allowed bail. [Footnote: History of Witchcraft; Upham.] He escaped and hurried to Duxbury, where he must have astonished his mother by the recital of his adventures. He left an estate of £2059, in his will, two houses, one of wood worth four hundred pounds, and another of brick worth two hundred and seventy pounds, besides much plate, brass and money and debts amounting to £1259, "the most of which are desperite." A tablet in the wall of the Old South Church at Copley Square, Boston, records his death at the age of seventy-five, March, 1701. He was an original member of this church. Perhaps Priscilla varied her peaceful life by visits to this affluent son in Boston. There is no evidence of the date of Priscilla Alden's death or the place of her burial. She was living and present, with her husband, at Josiah Winslow's funeral in 1680. She must have died before her husband, for in his Inventory, 1686, he makes no mention of her. He left a small estate of only a little over forty pounds, although he had given to his sons land in Duxbury, Taunton, Middleboro and Bridgewater. [Footnote: The Mayflower Descendant, iii, 10. The Story of a Pilgrim Family; Rev. John Alden; Boston, 1890.] Probably Priscilla also bestowed some of her treasures upon her children before she died. Some of her spoons, pewter and candle-sticks have been traced by inheritance. It is not likely that she was "rich in this world's goods" through her marriage, but she had a husband whose fidelity to state and religion have ever been respected. To his memory Rev. John Cotton wrote some elegiac verses; Justin Winsor has emphasized the honor which is still paid to the name of John Alden in Duxbury and Plymouth: [Footnote: History of Duxbury;

Winsor.] "He was possessed of a sound judgment and of talents which, though not brilliant, were by no means ordinary—decided, ardent, resolute, and persevering, indifferent to danger, a bold and hardy man, stern, austere and unyielding and of incorruptible integrity." The name of Mary Chilton is pleasant to the ear and imagination. Chilton Street and Chiltonville in Plymouth, and the Chilton Club in Boston, keep alive memories of this girl who was, by persistent tradition, the first woman who stepped upon the rock of landing at Plymouth harbor. This tradition was given in writing, in 1773, by Ann Taylor, the grandchild of Mary Chilton and John Winslow. [Footnote: History of Plymouth; James Thatcher.] Her father, James Chilton, sometimes with the Dutch spelling, Tgiltron, was a man of influence among the early leaders, but he died at Cape Cod, December 8, 1620. He came from Canterbury, England, to Holland. By the records on the Roll of Freemen of the City of Canterbury, [Footnote: Probably this freedom was given, by the city or some board therein, as mark of respect. N. E. Gen. Hist. Reg., 63, 201.] he is named as James Chylton, tailor, "Freeman by Gift, 1583." Earlier Chiltons,—William, spicer, and Nicholas, clerk,—are classified as "Freemen by Redemption." Three children were baptized in St. Paul's Church, Canterbury,—Isabella, 1586; Jane, 1589; and Ingle, 1599. Isabella was married in Leyden to Roger Chandler five years before *The Mayflower* sailed. Evidently, Mary bore the same name as an older sister whose burial is recorded at St. Martin's, Canterbury, in 1593. Isaac Chilton, a glass-maker, may have been brother or cousin of James. Of Mary's mother almost nothing has been found except mention of her death during the infection of 1621. [Footnote: Bradford's History of Plymouth Plantation; Appendix.]

When *The Fortune* arrived in November, 1621, it brought Mary Chilton's future husband among the passengers,—John Winslow, younger brother of Edward. Not later than 1627 they were married and lived at first in the central settlement, and later in Plain Dealing, North Plymouth. They had ten children. The son, John, was Brigadier-General in the Army. John Winslow, Sr., seemed to show a spirit of enterprise by the exchange and sale of his "lots" in Plymouth and afterwards in Boston where he moved his family, and became a successful owner and master of merchant ships. Here he acquired land on Devonshire Street and Spring Lane and also on Marshall Lane and Hanover Street. From Plans and Deeds, prepared by Annie Haven Thwing, [Footnote: Massachusetts Historical Society, Boston.

Also dimensions in Bowditch Title Books: 26: 315.] one may locate a home of Mary Chilton Winslow in Boston, a lot 72 and 85, 55 and 88, in the rear of the first Old South Church, at the southwest corner of Joyliffe's Lane, now Devonshire Street, and Spring Lane. It was adjacent to land owned by John Winthrop and Richard Parker. By John Winslow's will, probated May 21, 1674, he bequeathed this house, land, gardens and a goodly sum of money and shares of stock to his wife and children. The house and stable, with land, was inventoried for £490 and the entire estate for £2946-14-10. He had a Katch *Speedwell*, with cargoes of pork, sugar and tobacco, and a Barke *Mary*, whose produce was worth £209; these were to be divided among his children. His money was also to be divided, including 133 "peeces of eight." [Footnote: The Mayflower Descendant, 111, 129 (1901).]

Interesting as are the items of this will, which afford proofs that Mary Chilton as matron had luxuries undreamed of in the days of 1621, *her* will is even more important for us. It is one of the three *original* known wills of *Mayflower* passengers, the others being those of Edward Winslow and Peregrine White. Mary Chilton's will is in the Suffolk Registry of Probate, [Footnote: This will Is reprinted In The Mayflower Descendant, I: 85.] Boston, in good condition, on paper 18 by 14 inches. The will was made July 31, 1676. Among other interesting bequests are: to my daughter Sarah (Middlecot) "my Best gowne and Pettecoat and my silver beare bowl" and to each of her children "a silver cup with a handle." To her grandchild, William Payne, was left her "great silver Tankard" and to her granddaughter, Ann Gray, "a trunk of Linning" (linen) with bed, bolsters and ten pounds in money. Many silver spoons and "ruggs" were to be divided. To her grandchild, Susanna Latham, was definite allotment of "Petty coate with silke Lace." In the inventory one may find commentary upon the valuation of these goods—"silk gowns and pettecoats" for £6-10, twenty-two napkins at seven shillings, and three "great pewter dishes" and twenty small pieces of pewter for two pounds, six shillings. She had gowns, mantles, head bands, fourteen in number, seventeen linen caps, six white aprons, pocket-handkerchiefs and all other articles of dress. Mary Chilton Winslow could not write her name, but she made a very neat mark, M. She was buried beneath the Winslow coat of arms at the front of King's Chapel Burial-ground in Boston. She closely rivalled, if she did not surpass in wealth and social position, her sister-in-law, Susanna White Winslow.

Elizabeth Tilley had a more quiet life, but she excelled her associates among these girls of Plymouth in one way,—she could write her name very well. Possibly she was taught by her husband, John Howland who left, in his inventory, an ink-horn, and who wrote records and letters often for the colonists. For many years, until the discovery and printing of Bradford's History of Plymouth Plantation in 1856, it was assumed that Elizabeth Tilley was either the daughter or granddaughter of Governor Carver; such misstatement even appears upon the Howland tombstone in the old burying-ground at Plymouth. Efforts to explain by assuming a second marriage of Carver or a first marriage of Howland fail to convince, for, surely, such relationships would have been mentioned by Bradford, Winslow, Morton or Prence. After the death of her parents, during the first winter, Elizabeth remained with the Carver household until that was broken by death; afterwards she was included in the family over which John Howland was considered "head"; according to the grant of 1624 he was given an acre each for himself, Elizabeth Tilley, Desire Minter, and the boy, William Latham.

The step-mother of Elizabeth Tilley bore a Dutch name, Bridget Van De Veldt. [Footnote: N. E. Gen. Hist. Reg., i, 34.] Elizabeth was ten or twelve years younger than her husband, at least, for he was twenty-eight years old in 1620. They were married, probably, by 1623-4, for the second child, John, was born in 1626. It is not known how long Howland had been with the Pilgrims at Leyden; he may have come there with Cushman in 1620 or, possibly, he joined the company at Southampton. His ancestry is still in some doubt in spite of the efforts to trace it to one John Howland, "gentleman and citizen and salter" of London. [Footnote: Recollections of John Howland, etc. E. H. Stone, Providence, 1857.] Probably the outfit necessary for the voyage was furnished to him by Carver, and the debt was to be paid in some service, clerical or other; in no other sense was he a "servant." He signed the compact of *The Mayflower* and was one of the "ten principal men" chosen to select a site for the colony. For many years he was prominent in civic affairs of the state and church. He was among the liberals towards Quakers as were his brothers who came later to Marshfield,—Arthur and Henry. At Rocky Neck, near the Jones River in Kingston, as it is now called, the Howland household was prosperous, with nine children to keep Elizabeth Tilley's hands occupied. She lived until past eighty years, and died at the home of her daughter, Lydia Howland Brown, in Swanzey, in 1687. Among the articles mentioned in her will are many books of religious type. Her husband's estate as inventoried was not large, but mentioned such useful articles as silk neckcloths, four dozen buttons and many skeins of silk. [Footnote: The Mayflower Descendant, ii, 70.]

Constance or Constanta Hopkins was probably about the same age as Elizabeth Tilley, for she was married before 1627 to Nicholas Snow, who came in *The Ann*. They had twelve children, and among the names one recognizes such familiar patronymics of the two families as Mark, Stephen, Ruth and Elizabeth. Family tradition has ascribed beauty and patience to this maiden who, doubtless, served well both in her father's large family and in the community. Her step-sister, Damaris, married Jacob Cooke, son of the Pilgrim, Francis Cooke.

CHAPTER IV
COMPANIONS WHO ARRIVED IN THE FORTUNE AND THE ANN

After the arrival of *The Ann*, in the summer of 1623, the women who came in *The Mayflower* had more companions of good breeding and efficiency. Elizabeth Warren, wife of Richard, came with her five daughters; it is safe to assume the latter were attractive for, in a few years, all were well married. Two sons were born after Elizabeth arrived at Plymouth, Nathaniel and Joseph. For forty-five years she survived her husband, who had been a man of strength of character and usefulness as well as some wealth. When she died at the age of ninety-three leaving seventy-five great grandchildren, the old Plymouth Colony Records paid her tribute,—"Mistress Elizabeth Warren, haveing lived a Godly life came to her Grave as a Shock of corn full Ripe. She was honourably buried on the 24th of October (1673)."

Evidently, Mistress Warren was a woman of independent means and efficiency,—else she would have remarried, as was the custom of the times. She became one of the "purchasers" of the colony and conveyed land, at different times, near Eel River and what is now Warren's Cove, in Plymouth, to her sons-in-law. An interesting sidelight upon her character and home is found in the Court Records; [Footnote: I, 35, July 5, 1635.] her servant, Thomas Williams, was prosecuted for "speaking profane and blasphemous speeches against ye majestie of God. There being some dissension between him and his dame she, after other things, exhorted him to fear God and doe his duty."

Bridget Fuller followed her husband, Dr. Samuel, and came in *The Ann*. She also long survived her husband and did not remarry. She carried on his household and probably also his teaching for many years after he fell victim to the epidemic of infectious fever in 1633. She was his third wife, but only two children are known to have used the Fuller cradle, now preserved in Pilgrim Hall, Plymouth. It has been stated that, in addition to these two, Samuel and Mercy, another young child came with its mother in *The Ann*, but did not live long. [Footnote: Ancient Landmarks of Plymouth; W. T. Davis] The son, Samuel, born about 1625, was minister for many years at

Middleboro; he married Elizabeth Brewster, thus preserving two friendly families in kinship.

Evidently, Bridget Fuller was very ill and not expected to recover when her husband was dying, for in his will, made at that time, he arranged for the education of his children by his brother-in-law, William Wright, unless it "shall please God to recover my wife out of her weake estate of sickness." It is interesting also that, in this will, provision was made for the education of his daughter, Mercy, as well as his son, Samuel, by Mrs. Heeks or Hicks, the wife of Robert Hicks who came in *The Ann*. [Footnote: Plymouth Colony Wills and Inventories; also in The Mayflower Descendant, 1, 245.] Not alone for his own children did this good physician provide education, but also for others "put to him for schooling," — with special mention of Sarah Converse "left to me by her sick father." This kind, generous doctor left a considerable estate, in spite of the many "debts for physicke," including that of "Mr. Roger Williams which was freely given." One specific gift was for the good of the church and this forms the nucleus of a fund which is still known as the Fuller Ministerial Fund of the Plymouth Congregational Church. Its source was "the first cow calfe that his Brown Cow should have." [Footnote: Genealogy of Some Descendants of Dr. Samuel Fuller of *The Mayflower*, compiled by William Hyslop Fuller, Palmer.]

Mrs. Alice Morse Earle says that gloves were gifts of sentiment; [Footnote: Two Centuries of Costume in America; Alice Morse Earle; N. Y., 1903.] they were generously bestowed by this physician of old Plymouth. Money to buy gloves, or gloves, were bequeathed to Mistress Alice Bradford and Governor Winthrop of the Massachusetts Bay Colony; also to John Winslow, John Jenny and Rebecca Prence. The price allowed for a pair of gloves was from two to five shillings. Probably these may have been the fringed leather gloves or the knit gloves described by Mrs. Earle. Another bequest was his "best hat and band never worn to old Mr. William Brewster." To his wife was left not alone two houses, "one at Smeltriver and another in town," but also a fine supply of furnishings and clothes, including stuffe gown, red pettecoate, stomachers, aprons, shoes and kerchiefs. Mistress Fuller lived until after 1667, and exerted a strong influence upon the educational life of Plymouth.

Is it heresy to question whether the sampler, [Footnote: In Pilgrim Hall, Plymouth.] accredited to Lora or Lorea Standish, the daughter of Captain Miles and Barbara Standish, was not more probably the work of the granddaughter, Lorea, the child of Alexander Standish and Sarah Alden? The style and motto are more in accord with the work of the later generation and, surely, the necessary time and materials for such work would be more probable after the pioneer days. This later Lora married Abraham Sampson,

son of the Henry who came as a boy in *The Mayflower*. [Footnote: Notes to Bradford's History, edition 1912.] The embroidered cap [Footnote: In Pilgrim Hall, Plymouth.] and bib, supposed to have been made by Mistress Barbara for her daughter, would prove that she had

> *"hands with such convenient skill*
>
> *As to conduce to vertu void of shame"*

which were the aspiration of the girl who embroidered, or "wrought," the sampler. It is a pleasant commentary upon the tastes and industry of Mistress Barbara Standish that, amid the cares of a large family and farm, she found time for such dainty embroideries as we find in the cap and bib.

Probably two young sons of Captain and Barbara Standish, Charles and John, died in the infectious fever epidemic of 1633. A second Charles with his brothers, Alexander, Miles and Josiah, and his sister, Lorea, gladdened the hearth of the Standish home on Captain's Hill, Duxbury. A goodly estate was left at the death of Captain Miles, including a well-equipped house, cattle, mault mill, swords (as one would expect), sixteen pewter pieces and several books of classic literature,—Homer, Caesar's Commentaries, histories of Queen Elizabeth's reign, military histories, and three Bibles with commentaries upon religious matters. There were also medical books, for Standish was reputed to have been a student and practitioner in times of emergency in Duxbury. He suffered a painful illness at the close of his vigorous, adventuresome life. Perhaps Barbara needed, at times, grace to endure that "warm temper" which Pastor Robinson deplored in Miles Standish, a comment which the intrepid Captain forgave and answered by a bequest to the granddaughter of this loved pastor. We may be sure Barbara was proud of the mighty share which her husband had in saving Plymouth Colony from severe disaster, if not from extinction. It is surmised that Barbara Standish was buried in Connecticut where she lived during the last of her life with her son, Josiah. Possibly, however, she may have been buried beside her husband, sons, daughter and daughter-in-law, Mary Dingley, in Duxbury. [Footnote: Interesting facts on this subject may be found in "The Grave of Miles Standish and other Pilgrims," by E. V. J. Huiginn; Beverly, 1914.]

The Colonial Governor and his Lady ever held priority of rank. Such came to Mrs. Alice Southworth when she married Governor William Bradford a few days after her arrival on *The Ann*. Tradition has said persistently that this was the consummation of an earlier romance which was broken off by the marriage of Alice Carpenter to Edward Southworth in

Leyden. The death of her first husband left her with two sons, Thomas and Constant Southworth, who came to Plymouth before 1628. She had sisters in the Colony: Priscilla, the wife of William Wright, came in *The Fortune*; Dr. Fuller's first wife had been another sister; Juliana, wife of George Morton, was a third who came also in *The Ann*. Still another sister, Mary Carpenter, came later and lived in the Governor's family for many years. At her death in her ninety-first year, she was mourned as "a Godly old maid, never married." [Footnote: Hunter's Collections, 1854.]

The first home of the Bradfords in Plymouth was at Town Square where now stands the Bradford block. About 1627-8 they moved, for a part of the year, to the banks of the Jones River, now Kingston, a place which had strongly appealed to Bradford as a good site for the original settlement when the men were making their explorations in December, 1620. William, Joseph and Mercy were born to inherit from their parents the fine characters of both Governor and Alice Bradford, and also to pass on to their children the carved chests, wrought and carved chairs, case and knives, desk, silver spoons, fifty-one pewter dishes, five dozen napkins, three striped carpets, four Venice glasses, besides cattle and cooking utensils and many books. That the Governor had a proper "dress suit" was proved by the inventory of "stuffe suit with silver buttons and cloaks of violet, light colour and faced with taffety and linen throw."

As Mistress Bradford could only "make her mark," she probably did not appreciate the remarkable collection, for the times, of Latin, Greek, Hebrew, Dutch and French books as well as the studies in philosophy and theology which were in her husband's library. There is no doubt that the first and second generations of girls and boys in Plymouth Colony had elementary instruction, at least, under Dr. Fuller and Mrs. Hicks as well as by other teachers. Bradford, probably, would also attend to the education of his own family. The Governor's wife has been accredited with "labouring diligently for the improvement of the young women of Plymouth and to have been eminently worthy of her high position." [Footnote: The Pilgrim Republic; John A. Goodwin, p. 460.] She was the sole executrix of her husband's estate of £1005,—a proof of her ability.

Sometimes her cheerfulness must have been taxed to comfort her husband, as old age came upon him and he fell into the gloomy mood reflected in such lines as these: [Footnote: New England Memorial; Morton.]

"In fears and wants, through weal and woe,
A pilgrim passed I to and fro;

Oft left of them whom I did trust,
How vain it is to rest in dust!
A man of sorrows I have been,
And many changes I have seen,
Wars, wants, peace, plenty I have known,
And some advanc'd, others thrown down."

When Mistress Alice Bradford died she was "mourned, though aged" by many. To her memory, Nathaniel Morton, her nephew, wrote some lines which were more biographic than poetical, recalling her early life as an exile with her father from England for the truth's sake, her first marriage:

"To one whose grace and virtue did surpasse,
I mean good Edward Southworth whoe not long
Continued in this world the saints amonge."

With extravagant words he extols the name of Bradford,—"fresh in memory Which smeles with odoriferous fragrancye." This elegist records also that, after her second widowhood, she lived a

"life of holynes and faith,
In reading of God's word and contemplation
Which healped her to assurance of salvation."

This is not a very lively, graphic description of the woman most honored, perhaps, of all the pioneer women of Plymouth, but we may add, by imagination, a few sure traits of human kindliness and grace. She was typical of those women who came in *The Mayflower* and her sister ships. Although she escaped the tragic struggles and illness of that first winter, yet she revealed the same qualities of courage, good sense, fidelity and vision which were the watchwords of that group of women in Plymouth colony. Yes,—they had vision to see their part in the sincere purpose to establish a new standard of liberty in state and church, to serve God and mankind with all their integrity and resources.

As the leaders among the men were self-sacrificing and honorable in their dealings with their financiers, with the Indians and with each other, so the women were faithful and true in their homes and communal life. They took scarcely any part in the civic administration, for such responsibility did not come into the lives of seventeenth century women. They were actively interested in the educational and religious life of the colony. Their moral standards were high and inflexible; they extolled, and practised, the virtues of thrift and industry. It may be well for women in America today, who were querulous at the restrictions upon sugar and electric lights, to consider the good sense, and good cheer, with which these women of Plymouth Colony directed their thrifty households.

We would not assume that they were free from the whims and foibles of womankind,—and sometimes of man-kind,—of all ages. They were, doubtless, contradictory and impulsive at times; they could scold and they could gossip. We believe that they laughed sometimes, in the midst of dire want and anxiety, and we know that they prayed with sincerity and trust. They bore children gladly and they trained them "in the fear and admonition of the Lord." They were the progenitors of thousands of fine men and women in all parts of America today who honor the *women* as well as the *men* of the old Plymouth Colony,—the women who faithfully performed, without any serious discontent,

> *"that whole sweet round*
> *Of littles that large life compound."*

INDEX TO PERSONS MENTIONED IN THE TEXT

Lydia (Brown)
John
Huiginn, E. V. J.

Jenny, John
Jeppson, William
William
Jones, Christopher, Capt.
Thomas, Capt.

Latham, William
Lister, Edward
Longfellow, Henry W.
Lord, Arthur, VI

Martin, Mrs. Christopher
Masefield, John
Massasoit
Minter, Desire
John
Thomas
William
More, Ellen
Richard
Morton, George
Juliana Carpenter
Mullins, Alice, Mrs.
Joseph
Moses
Priscilla
Sarah (Blunden)
William
William, Jr.

Newcomen, John

Oldham, John

Pabodie, Elizabeth Alden
William
Parker, Richard
Penn, Christian
Prence, Thomas
Priest, Degory

Reynolds, William
Rigdale, Alice
Robinson, Pastor John

Sampson, Alexander
Henry
Samoset
Snow, Nicholas
Soule, George
Southworth, Alice
Constant
Thomas
Squanto
Standish, Alexander
Barbara
Charles
John
Josiah
Lora or Lorea
Mary Dingley
Miles
Miles, Jr.
Rose

Taylor, Ann
Thompson, Edward
Thwing, Annie M.
Tilley, Ann
Bridget
Edward

Elizabeth
John
Tinker, Mrs. Thomas
Turner, John

Warren, Elizabeth
Richard
White, Peregrine
Resolved
Susanna
William
Williams, Roger
Thomas
Winslow, Edward
Elizabeth Barker
Elizabeth
John
John, Brig. Gen.
Josiah
Kenelm
Mary Chilton
Susanna
Winthrop, John
Wright, Priscilla Carpenter
William

9 789359 328577